A QUICK INTERVENTION FOR ANXIETY

MY MAGICAL THREE THAT SETS ME FREE

DR. AREZOO KHANZADEH

ILLUSTRATED BY JOHN AND NEVIN BENEDICT

Archway Publishing books may be ordered through booksellers or by contacting:

Archway Publishing
1663 Liberty Drive
Bloomington, IN 47403
www.archwaypublishing.com
844.669.3957

Illustration credit: John & Nevin Benedict

ISBN: 978-1-4808-9428-0 (sc)
ISBN: 978-1-4808-9427-3 (hc)
ISBN: 978-1-4808-9429-7 (e)

Print information available on the last page.

Archway Publishing rev. date: 03/15/2021

This book is dedicated to:

All the little ones out there,
struggling with intense anxiety.
Keep glowing. Keep shining.
Like the bright star that you are!

One out of three children experience some level of anxiety. Anxiety cannot be seen, but when it is experienced, it can be intense and difficult to process through. This book is a small tool to be used with a therapist, school counselor, teacher, parent, or any caring adult in the child's life. The purpose of the book is to walk through the three main questions when experiencing a worry or intense anxiety. Is it solvable? Do I have the means to solve it? And is the time right to tackle the worry? With each question, the child can determine whether to let go of the worry or work it through.

I woke up this morning,
with my heart racing…
thumping and beating,
my brain is overthinking.

I cannot breathe,
what is happening to me?
My hands are shaking,
the room is spinning.
Anxiety takes over me.

I feel all…

tangled up by…

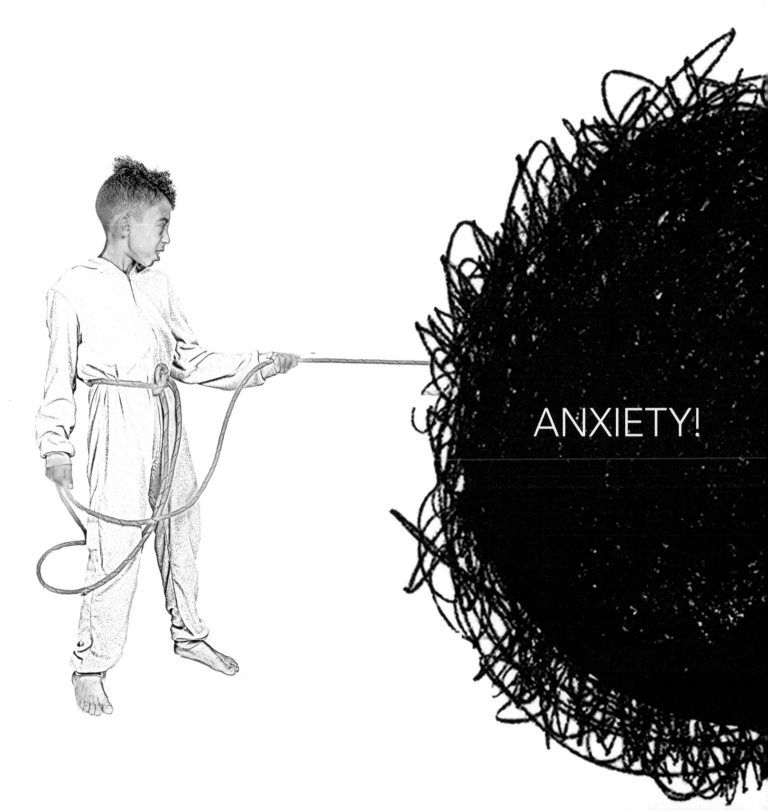

I immediately recalled
what Dr. Azy said to me.

"Do not fret little one,
let us count to three."

I stopped and I reflected.
Oh yes, the magical three.

The questions I ask myself,
to work through my anxiety.

1 I ask myself the first question…
Is my worry something I can fix?

Does it have a solution?
Or an answer I can pick?

If the answer is no I must let it go!

Let my worry go and fly away.
And set me free from anxiety.

2 I ask question two.

Do I have the tools to solve the issue?
To get me out of my heavy blues.

If the answer is no I must let it go!

Let my worry go and fly away.
And set me free from anxiety.

3 I have my solution and the tools to tackle my heavy blues.

But question three is the key, is the timing right for me?

If the answer to
all three questions
is a yes, then
I work it out…

Solve it and let my worry fade away.

But if the answers are all no,
then why stress?

I just let it go.

Printed in the United States
by Baker & Taylor Publisher Services